THE FIREWORK-MAKER'S DAUGHTER

Phillip Pullman

THE FIREWORK-MAKER'S DAUGHTER

Adapted for the stage by Stephen Russell

OBERON BOOKS
LONDON

First published in 2010 by Oberon Books Ltd
521 Caledonian Road, London N7 9RH
Tel: 020 7607 3637 / Fax: 020 7607 3629
e-mail: info@oberonbooks.com
www.oberonbooks.com

A catalogue record for this book is available from the British
Library.

ISBN: 978-1-84943-069-2

Cover Photography by Sophie O'Reirdan

Cover design by James Illman

Printed in Great Britain by CPI Antony Rowe, Chippenham.

The Birmingham Stage Company's production of
Philip Pullman's *The Firework-Maker's Daughter* was first
performed at The Everyman Theatre, Cheltenham on 20
October 2010 with the following cast:

LILA, Laura Durrant
CHULAK, Ben Wong
LALCHAND, Chris Talman
RAMBASHI, Craig Painting
GODDESS OF THE LAKE, Natasha Lewis
HAMLET THE ELEPHANT, Matt Williamson
HUNGRY PIRATE, Iwan Tudor
KING, Jak Poore
FRANGIPANI, Jennifer O'Neill
CROCODILE, Alexander Scott

Creative team

Adapted by Stephen Russell
Director, Phil Clark
Designer, Jackie Trousdale
Lighting, Jason Taylor
Music, Jak Poore
Sound, Mike Beer
Puppeteer, Toby Olie
Costume Supervisor, Gemma Hughes
Production Manager, Digby Robinson
CSM, Simon Sinfield
DSM, Judith Barrow
Sound Operator, Matt Gibson

Characters

LILA

CHULAK

LALCHAND

RAMBASHI

GODDESS OF THE LAKE

HAMLET THE ELEPHANT

HUNGRY PIRATE

KING

FRANGIPANI

CROCODILE

ACT 1

1 - LALCHAND'S WORKSHOP

LALCHAND's workshop. Workbenches, chemicals, rockets, etc. A fuse is laid leading to a firework. A scruffy and dirty girl, LILA, comes onstage. She carefully adds a tiny amount of delicate powder to the firework, thinks about it, adds a tiny bit more. She thinks "why not" and pours a load in. She steps back and lights the fuse. It burns quickly towards the firework. LILA takes cover offstage.

A man, LALCHAND the Firework-Maker, walks into the workshop. He watches the fuse for a moment, then stands on it, putting it out.

LALCHAND: Lila!

LILA returns.

LALCHAND: What's this?

LILA: A rudimentary experiment, father.

LALCHAND grunts.

LILA: A standard Java Light, with cloud powder instead of flowers of salt.

LALCHAND: (*Impressed.*) Have you given it a name?

LILA: Tumbling Demons.

LALCHAND: Excellent. If it works I'll put it in the New Year Festival display.

LILA: That's three of my fireworks in your display.

LALCHAND: I know, and I'll let everybody else know too, *if* I win.

LILA: *When* you win.

LALCHAND: From your mouth to the King's ears, eh?

LILA throws some matches to LALCHAND. LALCHAND strikes a match.

LILA: There's a poster in the market. They've announced the other competitors.

LALCHAND's interested and forgets about the lit match.

LALCHAND: Who do I have to beat this year?

LILA: The usual lot. The greatest firework-makers in the world.

LALCHAND: Who are the favourites?

LILA: Herr Puffenflasch, of course.

LALCHAND: The King likes him. Ouch!

The match burns LALCHAND's fingers.

LILA: The King loves him, but he can't win three years in a row.

LALCHAND lights another match, sets it to the fuse and steps back.

LILA: And there's an American - Colonel Sam Sparkington. No one knows anything about him.

LALCHAND: You know what the Americans are like, they never go anywhere unless they're sure they're going to win.

(re. firework.)

Did you put anything else in this?

LILA: A little scorpion oil.

LALCHAND: One drop or two?

LILA: A teaspoon.

LALCHAND: (*Horrified.*) A teaspoon!?

The firework explodes. LALCHAND and LILA have all but had the clothes blown off them.

LILA: That's too much, isn't it.

LALCHAND: You could've blown up the whole city! You don't know enough to use those ingredients.

LILA: If you made me your apprentice I'd learn about things like that.

LALCHAND: So it's my fault you nearly killed us, is it? You're such an ignorant girl!

LILA: I know about most things.

LALCHAND: What are the ingredients of fly-away powder?

LALCHAND waves his hand and creates a shower of sparks in the air.

LILA: I don't know that.

LALCHAND: Where do you find thunder-grains?

LALCHAND throws a thunder-grain at LILA's feet. It makes a loud bang. LILA jumps.

LILA: Or that.

LALCHAND: There's no limit to the things you don't know.

LILA: I know about the secret!

LALCHAND: What?

LILA: I know about the secret. The secret all Firework-Maker's have to know.

LALCHAND: What is it?

LILA: I don't know what it is. I just know there is one.

LALCHAND: That's different. Let's get this Tumbling Demon in a bucket of water.

LILA: Aren't you going to tell me what it is?

LALCHAND: No.

LILA: Why not?

LALCHAND: It's a secret.

LILA: Father? Please? Help me. How else will I become a Firework-Maker?

LALCHAND: Don't be silly, Lila.

LILA: I'm almost grown...

LALCHAND: And look at the state of you. Thank God your mother's dead. She'd die all over again if she saw you today. I should have sent you to my sister Jembavati. A dancer, that's the job for you.

LILA: I don't like dancing. I like fireworks.

LALCHAND: We all *like* them. It's not just big bangs and colours in the sky. It's a divine profession. You treat it like a cook mixing cakes.

LILA: Cooks don't blow up cities. I'm ready.

LALCHAND: You aren't.

LILA: Help me.

LALCHAND: No, Lila.

LILA's about to protest more. LALCHAND cuts her off.

LALCHAND: No! You'll never be ready! Listen to what I say - you aren't going to be a Firework-Maker.

LILA: What?

LALCHAND: Hair like a pit of vipers, fingers all stained and burned... I can't remember the last time you had any eyebrows. How am I going to find you a husband looking like that?

LILA: (*Horrified.*) A *husband?*

LALCHAND: Of course! You can't stay in my workshop for ever. You've got to get married.

LALCHAND and LILA stare at each other.

LILA: You want *that?* For *me?*

2 - A MARKET

A busy market with stalls, rickshaws, frog and cricket traders, snake charmers, beggars on trolleys, etc. pushes onto the stage around LALCHAND and LILA. LILA's in shock.

A huge White Elephant, Hamlet, appears in the market, with a boy, CHULAK, on his back. HAMLET creeps up on LILA, but she turns around before he can tap her on the shoulder. CHULAK and HAMLET are disappointed.

CHULAK: Breathing too loudly, Hamlet. Got to hold your breath!

HAMLET snorts, then has a quick check round to see if anyone's listening. He has two large adverts fly-posted onto his rump. One reads: EAT AT THE GOLDEN LANTERN. The other: CHANG LOVES LOTUS BLOSSOM - TRUE XXX.

HAMLET: Hello, Lila.

LILA: Hello, Hamlet.

HAMLET: (*re. adverts.*) Have you seen these? The obnoxious brat's turned me into a walking billboard.

CHULAK: Stop fussing. Chang gave me a whole rupee for the message to Lotus Blossom.

HAMLET: The filthy shame.

LILA: You charge people money to advertise on him?

CHULAK: It's a public service. It's lucky to have your name on a White Elephant.

(Pointed to HAMLET.)

They'd pay even more if they knew you were a talking White Elephant.

HAMLET: People don't stare enough? The boy would have me dancing in a tutu for half a rupee!

CHULAK: We were saving up to run away...

LILA: (*s/v.*) Chulak? Are you trying to lose your head? The King has spies everywhere.

They look round the market. A spy pops his head out of the snake charmer's basket. One of the beggars takes a photo. The King has spies everywhere.

CHULAK: It doesn't matter now, he doesn't want to go. He's fallen in love with a lady elephant at the zoo.

HAMLET: Frangipani.

Music plays. HAMLET looks wistful

HAMLET: Though she won't spare me the ghost of a dirty glance. Lila, I hope you never form an unrequited emotional attachment. There's no greater sadness...

LILA: I'm not sure about that.

HAMLET: Something ails you?

LILA: My father.

CHULAK: Old Lalchand? He's all right, isn't he? Not having trouble with his ticker again?

LILA: He doesn't want me to be a Firework-Maker.

CHULAK: Is that all?

LILA: It's serious. He's keeping something from me.

CHULAK: What?

LILA: The secret of firework-making. I've learned all about spark repellent, glimmer-juice and salts-of-shadow. And I'll learn about scorpion oil and thunder-grains. But there's something else. A special secret.

CHULAK: Tricky. Don't worry, I'll find it out.

LILA: Why would he tell you, when he won't tell me?

CHULAK: I'm too clever for him. He won't have a choice.

The laid-back ELEPHANT MASTER strolls into the market.

ELEPHANT MASTER: You've been at it again, haven't you Chulak?

CHULAK: (*innocently.*) At it, Master?

ELEPHANT MASTER: This Royal White Elephant is plastered in promotional materials.

CHULAK: I can't understand how it happens, Master.

ELEPHANT MASTER: It is your job to prevent this occurrence.

CHULAK: It's the traffic. I watch those rickshaw-drivers like a hawk. I can't look out for flyposters as well.

ELEPHANT MASTER: There's a good ten minutes work here. On a ladder.

CHULAK: It's a mystery, isn't it? Shall I clean them off?

ELEPHANT MASTER: I would, yes. The King has a job for his animal and he needs to be absolutely sparkling. Toe to tusk.

CHULAK starts to tear off the posters.

CHULAK: Who's the job?

ELEPHANT MASTER: Lord Parakit.

CHULAK: Lord Parakit? The Special and Particular Royal Toady?

ELEPHANT MASTER: He *was* the Special and Particular Royal Toady. Sacked.

CHULAK: But surely he's the finest sycophant in the world?

ELEPHANT MASTER: I'd've said so, he's done some magnificent grovelling.

Marching and trumpets are heard in the distance. The ELEPHANT MASTER is suddenly frightened and frenetic.

ELEPHANT MASTER: Quickly, Chulak! The King!

CHULAK finishes the job. The SPECIAL and PARTICULAR BODYGUARD marches into the market, knocking stalls out of the way.

SPECIAL AND PARTICULAR BODYGUARD: Prostrate yourselves before your sovereign!

All prostrate themselves as the KING (an austere and frightening man who commands immediate respect.) is carried into the market on a palanquin followed by an entourage which includes a cringing LORD PARAKIT.

LORD PARAKIT: Did I fail to flatter you sufficiently, Your Majesty? Would you like me to be more unctuous? Less unctuous? I can be any kind of toady you want...

KING: It's a great honour to have my noble White Elephant to stay, Lord Parakit. Don't you want to see that the King's pet has the very best your money can buy?

LORD PARAKIT looks sick.

LORD PARAKIT: Of course, Your Majesty.

KING: Good. He has many special requirements. He must bathe in tiger's milk every night...

LORD PARAKIT winces.

KING: He must have the finest yak wool carpets beneath his feet...

LORD PARAKIT sinks to his knees.

KING: And he must never step on the same carpet twice!

LORD PARAKIT whimpers. The Royal entourage exits.

HAMLET knocks over the barrel of frogs and bellows.

CHULAK: What're you doing, you vandal?

HAMLET: Another job. Another poor man to bankrupt. I hate Turkish Delight. I detest silk sheets. I loathe gold leaf on my tusks. I wish I was a normal dull grey elephant.

CHULAK: It's only Toady Parakit. It'll be fun.

HAMLET snorts derisively.

CHULAK: Are you sure you don't want to run away?

HAMLET: My heart belongs to Frangipani.

Music plays.

HAMLET: I must remain, despite my sorrows.

CHULAK sees LALCHAND.

CHULAK: Ah! There's your father.

LILA: He won't tell you.

CHULAK: Too clever. No choice.

3 - LALCHAND'S CART

CHULAK arrives at his close friend LALCHAND's cart.

LALCHAND: Chulak, street-urchin-who-leads-daughter-astray.

CHULAK: Lalchand, esteemed-father-of-wayward-friend.

LALCHAND: The White Elephant's going to Lord Parakit? How long will his money last?

CHULAK: A week.

LALCHAND: He's richer than I thought.

CHULAK: (*s/v.*) Between you and me, we might run away before then.

LALCHAND: (*s/v.*) Don't say that. You stupid boy. The King loves his elephant.

CHULAK: I've nearly got enough money to get us to India. We'll be safe there.

LALCHAND: Safe - maybe. Poor - definitely! How will you earn a living?

CHULAK: I thought I might do a bit of firework-making. Nice trade.

LALCHAND: Nice trade, my backside! Firework-making is an ancient and sacred art. You need talent, dedication and the favour of the gods to be a Firework-Maker.

CHULAK: All right, calm down. Remember the old...

(CHULAK pats his heart.)

It doesn't look difficult.

LALCHAND: Well it is.

CHULAK: How did you become one, then?

LALCHAND: I was apprenticed to my father for many years. Then I was tested to see if I had the Three Gifts.

CHULAK: Did you have them?

LALCHAND: Of course I did.

CHULAK: I've got more than three gifts.

LALCHAND: That's not all. There's an especially treacherous and dangerous part to the apprenticeship... that I can't tell you about.

CHULAK: That's a bit convenient, isn't it? Is it as dangerous as being stepped on by an elephant?

LALCHAND: Is it dangerous to travel to the Grotto of Razvani the Fire-Fiend, in the heart of Mount Merapi?

CHULAK: Mount Merapi, the volcano, famous for it's frequent and unpredictable eruptions of molten lava?

LALCHAND: Yes. That one.

CHULAK: Easy. I could do that.

LALCHAND: And is it easy to bring back...

> *(Confidential.)*

> Royal Sulphur?

CHULAK: What is...

> *(Confidential.)*

> Royal Sulphur?

LALCHAND: It's the prize ingredient for the finest fireworks. Without Royal Sulphur, no-one can ever be a true Firework-Maker.

CHULAK: And that's the special secret?

LALCHAND: Yes.

CHULAK: You're right. Firework-making's difficult and dangerous. I'll do something else.

LALCHAND: Good.

> *CHULAK starts to go.*

CHULAK: (*Business-like.*) Mount Merapi? Razvani the Fire-Fiend's Grotto? Royal Sulphur?

LALCHAND: Yes, you pestilential boy! And, hey, remember... It's a secret.

4 - A STREET

CHULAK lands next to LILA. All LILA's speech is drowned by fireworks as she flies into a rage.

CHULAK: He didn't tell you because he doesn't want you to get hurt.

> *LILA lets off a firework.*

CHULAK: Mount Merapi's dangerous. There's a Fire-Fiend...
Whatever that is.

More fireworks from LILA.

CHULAK: He told me because he had to. I told you he had no
choice.

Fireworks.

CHULAK: No, he doesn't think you're a child.

LILA leaves.

CHULAK: (*Calling after her.*) You've got to speak to him...

(To HAMLET.)

Oh no. I think I've made a terrible mistake. Why did I do
that, Hamlet?

HAMLET: Because you're an incorrigible show-off trying to
make up for your lowly station in life with frequent public
demonstrations of intellect.

CHULAK gives HAMLET a hard look.

HAMLET: Well you did ask.

5 - A MARKET

A piercing cry.

LALCHAND: Lila!

LALCHAND staggers into the market carrying a piece of paper.

LALCHAND: Lila!

(To fried-prawn seller.)

Have you seen, Lila?

The fried-prawn seller shakes his head.

LALCHAND: (*To batik-painter.*) Have you?

The batik-painter, likewise.

LALCHAND: Daughter! You don't know what you're doing!

Trumpets are heard. A procession approaches. A formally dressed CHULAK is driving the formally attired HAMLET (red silk, gold tusks, etc..) to LORD PARAKIT's mansion. LORD PARAKIT walks in front of the elephant, upset.

CHULAK: Royal White Elephant! Make way for the Royal White Elephant!

LORD PARAKIT: (*To HAMLET.*) Be a good beast. Don't eat me into poverty.

LALCHAND hurries to CHULAK and HAMLET.

LALCHAND: Did you tell Lila the secret?

CHULAK: What secret?

LALCHAND: *The* secret.

CHULAK: About Razvani and the Royal Sulphur? Course I did. Why?

LALCHAND: She's gone.

CHULAK: Gone where?

LALCHAND: To Mount Merapi - and she doesn't know the rest of it.

CHULAK: There's more?

LALCHAND: Of course there is. I would never betray the heart of my secret to a child like you! What have you done? No-one can go into the Fire-Fiend's Grotto without protection. She'll perish in the flames!

A blood-curdling roar from HAMLET. The entourage and market traders immediately scatter in terror. CHULAK climbs off HAMLET's back.

CHULAK: I didn't know... I thought I was helping her...

LALCHAND: You've sent her to her death.

HAMLET nudges the devastated CHULAK aside.

HAMLET: *(s/v.)* How can she be protected?

CHULAK: I don't know.

HAMLET: *(s/v.)* Ask Lalchand!

CHULAK: How can she be protected?

LALCHAND: It's too late...

CHULAK: Tell me!

LALCHAND: She needs magic water from the Goddess of the Emerald Lake.

CHULAK: The Emerald Lake's miles away. We can't possibly go there *and* catch up with Lila.

LALCHAND: She's doomed. It's all your fault.

CHULAK: I was trying to help...

HAMLET moves CHULAK to one side again.

HAMLET: *(s/v.)* There is one way - me. If we escape tonight, we could hurry the magic water to Lila. It's her only chance.

The servants and market traders are cautiously returning. CHULAK thinks for a moment, then leaps on the chance to redeem himself.

CHULAK: That's it! I was about to suggest that.

(To LALCHAND.)

I'll find her.

HAMLET bats CHULAK.

CHULAK: Me and Hamlet. We'll go tonight.

6 - A THICK JUNGLE

It's noisy - monkeys gibber, parrots screech, crocodiles snap their jaws. LILA pushes through the undergrowth. A snake hisses at her. LILA jumps out of the way and all but falls into a wide river.

LILA: Oh no! I'm a terrible swimmer... There's crocodiles down there...

LILA stands back from the river, dejected.

LILA: (*Steeling herself.*) I'm not turning back. I'll build a raft.

There's a rustle from some nearby vegetation. LILA's a little un-nerved. The bush rustles again. Suddenly, a huge man steps out of a different bush right next to LILA, causing her to jump.

RAMBASHI: River taxi, Miss?

LILA: You shouldn't jump out like that.

RAMBASHI: You want to cross the river?

LILA: I'm thinking about it.

RAMBASHI: I thought so. I saw that in a flash. And would I be correct in supposing that you had... money?

LILA: I might have a tiny little amount.

RAMBASHI: (*Disappointed.*) Just a little...

LILA: It's enough to pay your fare. Unless you're a complete crook?

RAMBASHI: A crook, miss? Me, miss? No, miss.

LILA fishes some coins out of her purse. As she opens the purse, RAMBASHI leans over and looks to see how much money she has. He's impressed. LILA hides the purse.

LILA: (*Offering money.*) One rupee. Take it or leave it.

RAMBASHI pretends to think about it for a moment.

RAMBASHI: Rambashi's River Taxi is delighted to be at your service.

(Bowing deeply.)

I am Rambashi.

RAMBASHI claps his hands. Out of the undergrowth come three scurvy dogs, CHANG, the LITTLE PIRATE and the HUNGRY PIRATE -dangerous-looking men with limbs missing, eye-patches and low brows. LILA's a little alarmed.

LILA: There's quite a lot of you, isn't there?

The pirates look baffled.

LITTLE PIRATE: It's a very fast taxi.

The pirates all laugh - then scowl at Lila. A boat is pulled from the undergrowth.

RAMBASHI: All aboard, all aboard. Set to it my brave lads.

They push the boat into the river. LILA's not sure about her decision now she's alone with the pirates.

CHANG: What's a young girl like you doing on her own out here? Don't you know it's dangerous?

LILA: I'm going to Mount Merapi.

LITTLE PIRATE: The volcano?

HUNGRY PIRATE: That's a long way. You'll need food for a journey like that?

LILA: I've hardly any.

HUNGRY PIRATE: No spare rice? No meat or vegetables?

LILA: No.

HUNGRY PIRATE: What about snacks between meals? Fruit? Chocolate? I can smell something tasty. Ow!

The HUNGRY PIRATE is hit on the head with an oar. It's clear they are very poor sailors.

LITTLE PIRATE: Concentrate. Stop thinking about your belly.

HUNGRY PIRATE: I'm too hungry to concentrate.

CHANG: You're pushing the stick the wrong way.

LITTLE PIRATE: It's called a paddle actually.

RAMBASHI: Think of the job in hand, lads.

All the pirates turn and look threateningly at LILA. LILA gulps. RAMBASHI's trailing his hand in the water behind the boat. LILA sees something approaching him.

LILA: Watch out! Crocodile!

RAMBASHI removes his hand from the snapping jaws of the crocodile. He leaps to his feet, terrified.

RAMBASHI: A sea monster! Run for your lives!

The boat almost capsizes as RAMBASHI rushes around.

LILA: Stand still you idiots! You'll capsize the boat!

RAMBASHI: Fight it, Chang!

CHANG: Me! Why?

LITTLE PIRATE: You're the biggest!

CHANG's pushed to the back of the boat and is about to hit the crocodile on the head with his oar when the HUNGRY PIRATE catches a crab and smacks him in the back with his oar. CHANG overbalances and jumps onto the crocodile's back.

CHANG: Help! Help me! Argh!

As CHANG precariously surfs the crocodile, the other men panic.

LILA: Pull him in! He'll be eaten!

Nobody knows what to do. LILA grabs an oar and rushes to the back of the boat.

LILA: Out of the way.

She smacks the crocodile with the oar. CHANG leaps back onto the boat in the nick of time.

LILA: That was a narrow squeak...

The boat cracks into the river bank. LILA is thrown into the bottom of the boat. The men recover first.

RAMBASHI: Quick lads.

CHANG: I don't want to now. She seems nice.

LITTLE PIRATE: And she's only a small girl.

RAMBASHI: We've got to start somewhere?

HUNGRY PIRATE: She's holding out on us. She's got food. That's the smell!

(*longingly.*)

Plum sauce.

The pirates all sniff the air lovingly.

CHANG: (*Salivating.*) Plum sauce.

LITTLE PIRATE: Let's do it.

The men put masks on their faces and pull out long knives. RAMBASHI has two, a curly one and a curved one.

RAMBASHI: Do I look fierce?

(*Being scary.*)

Argh!

The LITTLE PIRATE shrieks and cowers.

LITTLE PIRATE: (*Matter of fact.*) Not bad.

LILA climbs out of the bottom of the boat rubbing her head.

LILA: Ow. Have you lot ever been in a boat before? Oh...

RAMBASHI: Yes. Fooled you. Ha, ha! This isn't a River Taxi at all. We are pirates. We'd cut your throat as soon as look at you.

HUNGRY PIRATE: And drink your blood.

RAMBASHI: And drink your blood. Hand over your money, come on...

HUNGRY PIRATE: And eat your gizzard.

RAMBASHI: And eat...

(*To HUNGRY PIRATE.*)

We wouldn't do that.

(*To LILA.*)

You're captured. I warn you, we're desperate men.

LILA: That's completely obvious to anyone.

RAMBASHI: Bring the prisoner ashore.

LILA is pulled ashore by the LITTLE PIRATE.

HUNGRY PIRATE: Can't we eat some of her? I'm starving.

CHANG: You promised a hot meal every night.

RAMBASHI: How can we get a ransom if we eat her? You're a pack of scurvy dogs. Stop complaining.

RAMBASHI feints a punch at the complaining men.

RAMBASHI: (*To LILA.*) I hope you don't mind this little transaction? It's purely business.

LILA: Have you kidnapped me?

RAMBASHI: I'm afraid so. You're going to have to hand over all your money, and then we'll tie you up and hold you to ransom.

LILA: Have you done it before?

RAMBASHI: Yes, yes, yes. Many times.

LILA: What happens when you don't get any money?

HUNGRY PIRATE: We definitely eat you then.

RAMBASHI: Shhh.

LILA: You're not cannibals, are you?

HUNGRY PIRATE: We're really hungry.

LILA: Have you always been pirates?

RAMBASHI: No, I used to keep hens, but they all died of melancholy.

(*Sighing.*)

Poor hens... So I sold the business and bought the boat.

RAMBASHI steps back and pushes Lila in front of him.

RAMBASHI: Oh no! Ssh! Stop! Don't move! Ahh!

They all freeze. Ahead of them is thick vegetation. Nothing can be seen.

HUNGRY PIRATE: What is it? I can't see.

(*Excitedly moving forward.*)

It could be something tasty...

Suddenly, a huge tiger sticks its head out and roars loudly. RAMBASHI and his men are terrified. The HUNGRY PIRATE falls to the ground closest to the tiger.

LILA reaches into her bag and pulls out a firework. She pulls a pin and throws it at the tiger.

LILA: Stand back!

There's a huge bang and plume of smoke. The tiger yelps and flees. The pirates make the "ahhh" noise heard at firework displays.

LITTLE PIRATE: Pretty...

RAMBASHI recovers first.

RAMBASHI: Magnificent! Congratulations! I was about to stab him to death, of course, but never mind. What was that?

LILA: A self-igniting crackle-dragon. I made it.

RAMBASHI: You made it? I knew you were a talented girl. I saw that in a flash. We can't keep her hostage if she's saved our lives, can we lads?

LILA: Twice actually.

RAMBASHI: We can't keep her hostage if she's saved our lives twice, can we lads?

The lads agree.

RAMBASHI: You're now our honoured guest. We must have a feast!

HUNGRY PIRATE: We've no food.

RAMBASHI: Fish! Chang can catch some.

LITTLE PIRATE: I'm allergic to fish.

RAMBASHI: No, no, no, fish is *good* for you.

The boat has floated away.

CHANG: Where's the boat?

RAMBASHI: Who tied it up? Right that's it, I'm giving up crime. Fine pirates *you* are. I've got a better idea. Miss, can I interest you in a little investment?

LILA: No thank you. It's been interesting meeting you, but I'm on an important journey.

RAMBASHI: (*Not listening.*) This is a *much* better idea than piracy. It came to me in a flash. Can't fail.

LILA: It's dangerous, but I have to do it to become a real Firework-Maker...

LILA starts to walk slowly away as the pirates ignore her.

HUNGRY PIRATE: (*To RAMBASHI.*) Is there any food in it?

RAMBASHI: My dear boy. It's *built* on food.

LILA: Wish me luck.

RAMBASHI: (*Calling after LILA.*) I say! Miss! Don't go!

LILA turns back as she walks.

RAMBASHI: It's the safest investment you'll ever make! A million rupee idea!

7 - LORD PARAKIT'S GATES

HAMLET and CHULAK creep to the gate of LORD PARAKIT's house.

CHULAK: Do you think anyone heard us?

HAMLET: You forget, I'm a virtuoso creeper. They heard nothing. Can we escape past the Zoo?

CHULAK: Forget about Frangipani for now. We'll see her when we get back.

Music plays.

CHULAK: Stop that.

LALCHAND arrives with a tarpaulin.

LALCHAND: Psst! Chulak?

LALCHAND hands CHULAK a tarpaulin. CHULAK swirls it over HAMLET's head. HAMLET looks like a grey ghost.

CHULAK: You won't show up in the dark now.

HAMLET: It's terribly scratchy and it reeks of marquee. Couldn't you find a nice blanket?

CHULAK: Getting used to all that silken luxury after all?

LALCHAND: Help me up.

CHULAK: What? You're not coming.

LALCHAND: Why not?!

CHULAK: Hamlet's faster with one. And you're old with a weak heart.

LALCHAND: I must come!

CHULAK: You're slowing us down already.

LALCHAND slumps. Hamlet and Chulak set off.

LALCHAND: (*Calling after them.*) Keep my beautiful daughter safe.

Out of the shadows steps LORD PARAKIT.

LORD PARAKIT: You're Lalchand the Firework-Maker, aren't you?

LALCHAND starts with fright.

LALCHAND: Lord Parakit...

LORD PARAKIT: I've just seen you helping the White Elephant to escape.

LALCHAND: And you didn't stop me?

LORD PARAKIT: Why would I stop you? Do you know how much it *costs* to look after that elephant?

LALCHAND: So you're not going to tell the King?

8 - MOUNT MERAPI

LILA limps to the bottom of the volcano. She's scared. Her clothing is ripped and she looks a mess. She's come a long way.

LILA: It's quiet here... No birds or monkeys... Not like the jungle...

There's a deep and scary rumble from the volcano. LILA sits and looks at her foot.

LILA: I can feel that rumble in my chest...

LILA sucks at her foot.

LILA: I'll start my climb in the morning.

LILA wraps a blanket around herself and tries to get comfortable.

LILA: The air is cold, but the rocks are hot. I need a night in my own bed... With my father downstairs working late in the workshop...

LILA leaps to her feet and throws off her blanket in a sudden rage against her nostalgia.

LILA: This ground is too hard. I'll never sleep. I might as well climb.

LILA looks up, then screams and leaps out of the way. A shower of burning rocks fall from the mountain. They just miss her and lie on the floor glowing red. LILA's nerve goes. She starts to stagger away.

LILA: It's too dangerous... I could die in this lonely place.

LALCHAND in his workshop.

LALCHAND: You'll never be ready! Listen to what I say - you aren't going to be a Firework-Maker.

LILA steels herself - she won't be beaten. She turns back to the volcano and starts to climb.

9 - RAMBASHI'S JUNGLE GRILL

A restaurant in the jungle with RAMBASHI, CHANG, the HUNGRY and LITTLE PIRATES.

SONG AND DANCE: Rambashi's Jungle Grill.

RAMBASHI breaks off from the song as the restaurant catches fire.

RAMBASHI: What a splendid sight! Do you know, my boys, that gives me my best idea yet. It's just come to me in a flash.

CHULAK and HAMLET hurry into the clearing.

RAMBASHI: Chulak! My dear boy! How delightful to see you. What're you doing here?

CHULAK: Hello Uncle Rambashi. We're going to the Emerald Lake.

RAMBASHI: For the Ceremony of the Full Moon?

CHULAK: Yes.

RAMBASHI: It's over-rated. Don't bother. Stay with me. I've had a fantastic idea. You'd be perfect for it.

CHULAK: Sorry Uncle. We're in a hurry.

HUNGRY PIRATE: When do we get some food?!

RAMBASHI: (*Calling after HAMLET and CHULAK.*) It's a solid gold investment! A million rupee idea!

10 - MOUNT MERAPI

LILA has climbed high up the volcano.

LILA: How much further can it be... My fingers and toes are red raw... I've had worse burns than these making fireworks...

LILA slips and loses a shoe and her bag. They fall for a long time before they're heard smacking against the ground.

LILA: That was silly. Look where you're putting your feet, Lila, you clumsy clot!

LILA climbs on.

LILA: It's a long way down. But I won't look. I won't look. I won't...

LILA looks.

LILA: It's not that bad... I feel safer now. Father calls me...

LALCHAND in his workshop.

LALCHAND: Clumsy clot.

LILA: He wouldn't say that if he could see me here. I'm
practically a mountain goat -

There's a scream as LILA slips and falls from the volcano.

11 - THE EMERALD LAKE

*A small voice shouts, "Moon!". The moon is full, large and red. Villagers
and a HIGH PRIEST shuffle to the edge of the lake chanting. Ghostly
music plays under the chanting. The HIGH PRIEST walks to the edge
of the shore.*

HIGH PRIEST: Oh Goddess of the Emerald Lake we humbly
beseech thee to appear unto us!

*The GODDESS rises out of the water, as high as possible. She
shimmers. The crowd fall to their knees, awed by her presence.*

GODDESS: People of the Lake! The Goddess awaits. Come
with your requests. I'll be kind to those that are deserving,
but take care not to anger me. Those who are greedy or
frivolous - beware!

The HIGH PRIEST pushes a villager to the water's edge.

VILLAGER 1: Goddess, hear my plea...

The Goddess silences him, holding up her hand.

GODDESS: Your wish is just. Granted.

VILLAGER 1: Truly?

GODDESS: Truly.

*The VILLAGER runs to his girlfriend and hugs her. HAMLET and
CHULAK arrive.*

CHULAK: There she is. Shall I ask her?

HAMLET: Don't be so impetuous. Wait and see.

Another VILLAGER arrives at the water's edge.

VILLAGER 2: Goddess, hear my plea.

The GODDESS ponders for a moment.

GODDESS: Weren't you listening? The Goddess doesn't like to hear greedy requests. You've already got two.

VILLAGER 2: Yes, but one of them's got a faulty udder.

GODDESS: No. Your wish is rejected!

VILLAGER 2: I only wanted two cows-

VILLAGER 2 screams as he flies into the air and into the water.

CHULAK: Hey! I didn't know that could happen.

HAMLET: Now's the time, Chulak. Go forward and ask.

CHULAK: Aren't you watching? Look what happened to him.

HAMLET: Do it!

CHULAK: All right.

CHULAK reluctantly goes forward.

CHULAK: Goddess. Hear my plea.

Immediately, CHULAK is surrounded by villagers who grab his arms. Shouts ring out, "What are you doing, stranger?" "Away with him!" "Defiling the lake!" "Who is he? Who gave him permission?" "Stone him!" "Turn him out!"

CHULAK: I've got a special request for the Goddess!

HIGH PRIEST: How dare you come to this sacred place? The Goddess of the lake is not to be disturbed by you. Take him to the village boundary, and if he comes back, kill him!

HAMLET bellows and looks belligerent.

GODDESS: Villagers! The Goddess will decide who she sees. Let the boy free. Come forward.

CHULAK goes to the shore.

GODDESS: Bring the elephant.

HAMLET comes down to the water too.

GODDESS: What's that on his back?

HAMLET turns round and shows the adverts.

CHULAK: I thought I'd got rid of those.

GODDESS: Take them off. The elephant's too wise and noble to be advertised on. If he could speak I'm sure he'd tell you that himself.

HAMLET preens as CHULAK tears off the posters.

GODDESS: I know your wish. You want magic water?

CHULAK: Our friend didn't know she needed it to protect her in the Fire-Fiend's Grotto. All she wants is to get the Royal Sulphur so she can be a Firework-Maker. We don't want her to get hurt.

GODDESS: You should have thought about that before you opened your mouth then, shouldn't you?

CHULAK: I wasn't to know...

GODDESS: It's your fault your friend's in danger.

CHULAK: No, it's not.

GODDESS: It certainly is.

The GODDESS points at CHULAK.

GODDESS: You're an arrogant and thoughtless boy. Your wish is...

CHULAK closes his eyes and braces himself ready to be cast into the lake.

GODDESS: Granted.

The GODDESS throws a beam of light across the lake. A silver flask lands in CHULAK's hand. The GODDESS sinks quickly into the water. CHULAK opens his eyes and sees the flask.

HAMLET: Bravely done, Chulak. Quickly - on my back.

CHULAK: Can we get there in time?

HAMLET: I don't know, but we'll go so fast you'll believe an elephant can fly. Almost literally.

12 - RAZVANI'S GROTTO

LILA's fall ends as she lands in the grotto of RAZVANI the Fire-Fiend. She's stunned for a moment. Standing over her is the terrifying figure of RAZVANI the Fire-Fiend, the God of Fire. LILA's startled and scared by him.

LILA: (*Recovering.*) Is this the Grotto? Are you the Fire-Fiend?

RAZVANI: I am Razvani! The God of Fire!

LILA: I'm Lila, daughter of Lalchand-

RAZVANI: Why have you come to this place of flames?

LILA: I want to be a Firework-Maker.

RAZVANI: You!

LILA: Yes... I've come for Royal Sulphur.

RAZVANI: Where are the Three Gifts?

LILA: What Three Gifts? I don't know anything about them.

RAZVANI: What are you going to exchange for the Royal Sulphur?

LILA: I didn't know I was supposed to bring gifts. I'm sorry. I have come quite a long way.

RAZVANI claps his hands. A burning, smoking crevice rents the stage in two. LILA screams as she recoils from the heat.

LILA: I won't leave without the Royal Sulphur. Please, Razvani. I deserve it. I'll do anything. Show me what you want.

RAZVANI moves to the other end of the crevice from LILA.

RAZVANI: You want Royal Sulphur, walk through my fire!

LILA: Through there? But how? That's impossible.

RAMBASHI: Every true Firework-Maker's passed this test. Are you a true Firework-Maker?

LILA walks towards the flames.

LILA: It's too hot. I'll burn to cinders.

RAZVANI: Where's your magic water?

LILA: My what?

RAZVANI: No Three Gifts and no magic water?

LILA: I don't know about magic water or the Three Gifts. I will be a Firework-Maker. A good one. I invented self-igniting Crackle Dragons and Shimmering Coins. I've learned nearly everything my father could teach me.

RAZVANI: You haven't learned enough! Ghosts!

GHOST 1 appears.

GHOST 1: I too came without the Three Gifts. I burned so badly...

LILA backs away in fear. GHOST 2 surprises LILA.

GHOST 2: Take heed. I hadn't worked at the craft. I wasn't ready. The fire licked my limbs... The pain... Help me...

GHOST 3 appears.

GHOST 3: Maiden, turn back! You're like me. Headstrong. I had no water from the Goddess. I died... In flames. Don't join me... Turn back!

LILA's terrified.

LILA: I'm not like them. I don't care what anyone says. I am ready. Give me the Royal Sulphur.

RAZVANI: Receive it from my hands. Submit yourself as they did.

LILA's hesitating. She holds her hands in front of her face as the heat scorches her.

RAZVANI: Your father did it. Why are you waiting? I thought you wanted to be a Firework-Maker?

LILA: That's all I want.

RAZVANI: Then you must prove yourself.

LILA girds herself.

RAZVANI: You want to be a Firework-Maker? Walk into my flames!

LILA screws up her courage and walks into the flames. She immediately screams out in pain. She's starting to burn.

LILA: Help. Help me. Razvani? I'm burning.

She's surely dead.

HAMLET and CHULAK fly into the Grotto. The heat is too much for them. CHULAK runs as close as he can.

CHULAK: Lila! The water! Catch it!

CHULAK throws the flask of magic water. LILA catches it, but it's too late. She sinks into the flames. RAZVANI disappears. HAMLET and CHULAK stand back from the roaring heat.

CHULAK: Lila!

There's no sign of her.

CHULAK: Lila!

CHULAK goes to the pit but the heat forces him back. HAMLET grabs him and pulls him away.

HAMLET: Come back. You'll die too.

CHULAK sinks to the ground.

CHULAK: She's dead.

HAMLET puts a friendly trunk around CHULAK.

HAMLET: We came as fast as we could.

CHULAK: I've killed my friend. What a horrible death. What have I done?

HAMLET: You couldn't have known...

CHULAK: It's my fault! It's me that's done this... Lila! I'm so sorry!

HAMLET: Come away. She wouldn't want you to perish too.

Slowly, LILA rises from the burning crevice. She's unhurt and appears to be bathing in the flames.

CHULAK: Lila?

LILA looks at them and smiles. There's an explosion. The fire goes out. LILA steps out.

CHULAK: Are you all right?

LILA's stunned.

LILA: I'm fine, I think.

CHULAK: We thought you'd been killed.

LILA: Where's Razvani?

CHULAK: Who?

LILA: The Fire-Fiend? He was here.

HAMLET: We didn't see anyone.

LILA: But... He's got my Royal Sulphur. Razvani! I walked into the flames! Give me my Royal Sulphur!

CHULAK nudges HAMLET.

CHULAK: Tell her.

LILA: You've cheated me!

HAMLET: Lila, we've brought bad news. We've had a message from the city...

CHULAK: Lalchand was seen helping Hamlet escape.

HAMLET: The King's placed him under arrest.

CHULAK: He's going to be executed.

ACT 2

1 - THE KING'S PALACE

CHULAK and LILA are lying on the floor in the King's palace with HAMLET behind them. The SPECIAL AND PARTICULAR BODYGUARD has his foot on CHULAK's neck.

LILA: Will the King be long?

SPECIAL AND PARTICULAR BODYGUARD: Why? Is he keeping you waiting? Have you got another appointment?

LILA: No...

CHULAK: It's just the old... Argh. Foot on the neck thing. Beginning to hurt.

SPECIAL AND PARTICULAR BODYGUARD: Good.

LILA: We've come on a long and dangerous journey at great speed.

CHULAK: By elephant. Not a comfortable way to travel. Sorry Hamlet. Couldn't we have some water? Or some food even?

SPECIAL AND PARTICULAR BODYGUARD: Shut up, boy! I hope the King's in an imaginative mood when it comes to punishing you. I'll look forward to that.

Trumpets announce the KING's imminent arrival.

SPECIAL AND PARTICULAR BODYGUARD: Silence for the King!

The KING enters. LILA can't contain herself.

LILA: Have you killed my father?

SPECIAL AND PARTICULAR BODYGUARD: Speak to the King only when he speaks to you!

The SPECIAL AND PARTICULAR BODYGUARD cracks a whip by LILA's head.

SPECIAL AND PARTICULAR BODYGUARD: Faces to the ground! Especially you, boy.

CHULAK: Lower than this? Ahh...

The SPECIAL AND PARTICULAR BODYGUARD applies more pressure to CHULAK's neck.

KING: Your father will die tomorrow morning. There is only one penalty for what he has done.

LILA: Please spare him! It was my fault! I ran away without telling him...

SPECIAL AND PARTICULAR BODYGUARD: The King has spoken.

The SPECIAL AND PARTICULAR BODYGUARD cracks the whip again.

KING: Who's that?

CHULAK: Chulak, your Majesty... Ahhh!

The SPECIAL AND PARTICULAR BODYGUARD applies pressure.

SPECIAL AND PARTICULAR BODYGUARD: He's the Royal White Elephant's Special and Particular Groom, your Majesty.

KING: Let him speak.

CHULAK: Can I look up? It's not easy to talk with a foot on your neck.

The KING waves a hand. CHULAK climbs to his feet.

CHULAK: Your Majesty, as soon as I found out he'd escaped I swam across the river and I climbed mountains and fought my way through the jungle and, ow...

HAMLET whacks CHULAK out of the way with his trunk.

CHULAK: Stop that Hamlet...

Suddenly, HAMLET rushes forward, picks the SPECIAL AND PARTICULAR BODYGUARD up and throws him out of the window.

HAMLET: Your Majesty, could I possibly have a private word?

The KING is astonished.

KING: It's talking!

HAMLET: I appreciate it might be a shock, but not many people know. For a talking elephant I'm far from loquacious.

KING: And it's using big words!

The KING recovers his composure. HAMLET bows low.

HAMLET: Your Majesty... Forgive me. I humbly request a private audience.

KING: The White Elephant is a rare and wondrous beast. The request is granted...

The KING and HAMLET have a private talk. LILA climbs to her feet.

LILA: The King will never spare my father.

CHULAK: Hamlet's working on something...

LILA: He's an elephant! Why would the King listen to him?

CHULAK: He's a very persuasive elephant.

The battered SPECIAL AND PARTICULAR BODYGUARD comes back in.

SPECIAL AND PARTICULAR BODYGUARD: Where's the beast?

CHULAK: He's chatting to the King.

SPECIAL AND PARTICULAR BODYGUARD: I've had as much insolence as I'm going to take off you boy.

CHULAK: No really, he is. And the King's talking back too.

The SPECIAL AND PARTICULAR BODYGUARD tries to draw his sword but it's too bent to leave the scabbard. The KING and HAMLET return from their conference. HAMLET's looking very stern.

SPECIAL AND PARTICULAR BODYGUARD: Your majesty. This boy has defamed you. He says you've been talking to the elephant.

KING: (*Instantly angry.*) On your knees!

The SPECIAL AND PARTICULAR BODYGUARD falls to his knees.

KING: I decide who gets punished. Fetch the Special and Particular Royal Town Crier. I have a proclamation to make.

The SPECIAL AND PARTICULAR BODYGUARD starts to crawl out of the room.

KING: Quickly!

The SPECIAL AND PARTICULAR BODYGUARD jumps out of the window to please the KING.

KING: After careful consideration, I've made a wise and just decision. Firstly, elephants, do not talk.

LILA and CHULAK look to HAMLET. He stares ahead.

KING: (*To CHULAK.*) For allowing the White Elephant to escape, you are dismissed.

CHULAK sinks.

KING: Next week, is the New Year Festival firework competition. I have invited the greatest artists in fireworks from all over the world to show their displays. This year there will be a new entrant - you. The prize will go to the artist whose display receives the longest applause. That is all the other competitors will know. You will know something more. If your display wins, Lalchand will go free. Lose... and Lalchand dies!

2 - LALCHAND'S WORKSHOP

A fuse burns across the floor of the workshop. It reaches a large firework. There's a tiny bang.

CHULAK: Very disappointing. Come on, Lila, you've got to do better than that.

LILA: I wasn't testing the firework. I was testing the fuse.

CHULAK: (*Covering ignorance.*) Ah, I knew that actually... Did it work?

LILA: No. I need new fuses. Fuses that burn at different speeds so I can set off fireworks in stages. I think I can do it. In the jungle, creepers twisted round trees. Something like that might work...

CHULAK: (*Bemused.*) Yeah, it might... Nice.

LILA: I need new fireworks too. Things people have never seen before. More spectacle, louder explosions, brighter colours, higher rockets.

CHULAK: Sounds good. You seem to have everything in hand. I'm very impressed.

LILA sinks, depressed.

CHULAK: What's the matter?

LILA: I've no idea what I'm doing.

CHULAK: You've gone to a lot of trouble if you don't know what you're doing. Why did you climb Mount Merapi?

LILA: To be a Firework-Maker.

CHULAK: You're making fireworks.

LILA: There's too much to learn.

CHULAK: Well you'd better learn quickly. For Lalchand's sake.

LILA: I'm up against the greatest Firework-Makers in the world, in a competition that my father, who has thirty years of experience and taught me everything I know, has never won. If I don't win, he dies. I'm allowed to panic.

CHULAK: When you put it like that.

LILA turns over the cart of fireworks, scattering them across the stage.

CHULAK: Don't do that!

CHULAK hurries to pick up the fireworks.

LILA: I don't stand a chance.

CHULAK: You'll have the best... fuses.

LILA: I need my Royal Sulphur! If I had that...

CHULAK: You don't need it, I'll help you.

LILA: You? What every Firework-Maker needs - an unemployed elephant keeper.

CHULAK: I'm trying... I could make some of the simpler fireworks?

LILA: How do you make a Java light? That's simple.

CHULAK: I'm quick. You tell me what to do, I'll do it.

LILA: Teaching you will hold me up. You're completely useless.

CHULAK: Useless...

LILA: Leave me alone.

CHULAK: I could help. I could cook. Stay up late, keep you company. Tell you how well you're doing, but I'm useless... I'll go...

CHULAK leaves, hurt. LILA follows.

LILA: (*Calling.*) Chulak? Sorry. Come back... What's the use? My father is as good as dead.

3 - PRISON

High above the stage, LALCHAND lies in a suspended cage. CHULAK sneaks into a courtyard and checks no one is around. He whistles. HAMLET follows wearing the tarpaulin with the eyeholes cut out.

CHULAK: Why aren't you speaking to me? I've got the right elephant, haven't I? You are Hamlet.

HAMLET nods.

CHULAK: I've gone to a lot of trouble to get you here. You could be a bit pleased to see me?

HAMLET turns away, clearly not playing.

CHULAK: Have I done something to offend you?

HAMLET shakes his head.

CHULAK: Is it something to do with the King?

HAMLET nods vigorously.

CHULAK: Can you write it down?

HAMLET: You want me to write as well? I'm already very gifted for an elephant, you know?

CHULAK: I knew I could make you speak.

HAMLET: It's nothing to do with you. The King agreed to give Lalchand another chance in exchange for my silence.

CHULAK: So why are you speaking?

HAMLET: I'm in disguise.

CHULAK: Good point. Let's get into position.

CHULAK leaps onto HAMLET's shoulders and stretches to LALCHAND's cage. He can't reach.

CHULAK: Higher Hamlet.

HAMLET: This is as high as I go. Unless I stand on a ball like a circus freak?

CHULAK: Shush... Did you hear that?

HAMLET: What?

Four pairs of eyes are surrounding them.

CHULAK: Hello?

HUNGRY PIRATE: (*Singing barber shop style.*) Hello...

CHANG: (*Singing barber shop style.*) Hello...

LITTLE PIRATE: (*Singing barber shop style.*) Hello.

RAMBASHI leaps out of the dark.

RAMBASHI: Chulak! My dear boy!

(*Sings.*)

Hello...

CHULAK: Uncle Rambashi? What are you doing here?

RAMBASHI: We've come to the city to make our fortune.

CHULAK: Why were you singing?

RAMBASHI: My new idea. It came to me in a flash. We're entertainers. What do you think? A million rupee idea for sure?

CHULAK: Do you only do singing?

RAMBASHI: Only singing? Didn't you hear? We're entertainers! We do everything.

CHULAK: Do you do tumbling?

RAMBASHI: Tumbling?

CHULAK: You know, acrobatics?

RAMBASHI: Acrobatics? Yes, yes, yes! My brave lads will do anything for their audience.

The brave lads don't look too sure.

CHANG: Acrobatics? We don't do that, do we? Sounds dangerous?

LITTLE PIRATE: I thought we were singers?

HUNGRY PIRATE: I don't care as long as there's a hot juicy bite at the end. Or even a cold dry bite.

CHULAK takes RAMBASHI to one side.

CHULAK: Uncle? Do you think you could do me an acrobatic favour?

RAMBASHI: An acrobatic favour? You're sure you don't want a singing favour?

CHULAK: I need to get up there.

CHULAK points to LALCHAND's cage. RAMBASHI hardly hesitates at all.

RAMBASHI: Boys! Form a pointed thingy!

LITTLE PIRATE: A what?

RAMBASHI: Step to it!

CHANG: Step to what?

RAMBASHI: Three at the bottom, two on top. That's right. Come on. Use this excellent disguised elephant as a base.

HAMLET, RAMBASHI and the boys form a very dodgy and unstable pyramid.

RAMBASHI: Hold still boys! That's it!

CHULAK tries to climb to the summit but the pyramid keeps moving. When he makes it to the top, the pyramid becomes particularly unstable. CHULAK is now high enough to reach LALCHAND's cage but the pyramid keeps moving.

CHULAK: Hold it steady! Forward a little... Nearly there.

The pyramid suddenly flies forward. CHULAK grabs the cage and is left swinging in mid-air from the bars as HAMLET and the boys crash noisily off stage.

CHULAK: Esteemed-father-of-wayward-friend?

LALCHAND wakes.

LALCHAND: Chulak!

LALCHAND grabs CHULAK and pulls him up.

LALCHAND: Street-urchin-who-leads-daughter-astray... I never thought I'd be this pleased to see you. How's Lila?

CHULAK: She's alright. Moody and ungrateful, but alright.

LALCHAND: Is she ready for the competition?

CHULAK: I don't want to worry you, it being your life at stake and everything, but she doesn't think she can do it.

LALCHAND: Of course she can.

CHULAK: That's what I said, but she needs your help.

LALCHAND: Nonsense! She's a much better Firework-Maker than me!

CHULAK: Is she?

LALCHAND: Don't tell her that. I mean, it's not the right time. She has a flair... And what an imagination.

CHULAK: Why didn't you tell her that? Look where you are now.

LALCHAND hangs his head in shame.

LALCHAND: I've been foolish. Lila's grown while I haven't been watching. I wanted her to do things my way. I've been stubborn. And jealous.

CHULAK: Jealous?

LALCHAND: I should have been happy for her. I've got what I deserve.

CHULAK: Can Lila win the competition?

LALCHAND: It'll be difficult...

CHULAK: She's lost her confidence. Razvani didn't give her any Royal Sulphur. She doesn't think she stands a chance without it.

LALCHAND: She doesn't need Royal Sulphur.

CHULAK: That's not what she thinks.

LALCHAND: She doesn't. I can help her. I need to write a message.

4 - LALCHAND'S WORKSHOP

LILA's testing a firework. She lights a fuse and stands well back.

CHULAK: Lila! Lila!

CHULAK abseils down from the cage and straight into the firework.

LILA: What are you doing?! It's about to go off.

The firework explodes. CHULAK runs around, screaming.

CHULAK: Has it stopped?

LILA: Yes.

A final explosion causes CHULAK to jump.

LILA: Apart from that one.

CHULAK: I'm really sorry. Have I ruined your experiment?

He has, but LILA's pleased to see him.

LILA: It wouldn't have been very good without you running around. You've done me a favour.

CHULAK: Really?

LILA: Really.

CHULAK: So I'm not totally useless.

LILA: (*Apologising.*) Not totally useless. Let's say - almost totally useless... Will you stay? Help me? If you're not busy?

CHULAK: I'm not that busy.

LILA: Thank you.

CHULAK: Hey, I almost forgot.

(*Rummaging.*)

I've got this... from Lalchand.

CHULAK pulls out a charred and smoking letter. LILA takes it from him and reads it.

CHULAK: What does he say?

LILA: He says...

LALCHAND's in his cage.

LALCHAND: Dearest Daughter, I hope you can forgive me...

LILA: What for?

LALCHAND: I should have told you the secret of firework-making. I know you will create a magnificent display. Your loving father, Lalchand.

CHULAK: (*Unimpressed.*) Is that it?

LALCHAND: P.S. I'm sure you won't need it, but you can use my supply of Royal Sulphur. It's in a golden pot with a green lid on the bottom shelf of the gunpowder cupboard.

LILA dashes over to the workbench and starts frantically searching. She takes out the pot and opens it.

LILA: This?

She dabs a little powder on her finger and sniffs it.

LILA: This can't be it.

LILA checks the letter.

LALCHAND: P.P.S. add a pinch to each firework.

LILA puts a little Royal Sulphur on her tongue.

CHULAK: Is it Royal Sulphur?

LILA: That's what my father says. My dear father.

CHULAK: You know what this means? You can win.

LILA: Does it?

CHULAK: You've got the secret ingredient, haven't you?

LILA: I have.

(*Realising.*)

I have. I might be able to save him.

CHULAK: Of course you can!

LILA: Come on Chulak, there's work to be done. Stop being lazy.

CHULAK: You want me to help?

LILA: You're the best assistant I've ever had.

CHULAK: I'm the only assistant you've ever had.

LILA and CHULAK start mixing powders and loading their cart as the other Firework-Makers start to arrive on stage and set up their displays.

5 - THE NEW YEAR FESTIVAL

It's the second day of the New Year Festival. HERR PUFFENFLASCH stands by a huge model of a prawn. COLONEL SAM SPARKINGTON is helping to push a huge rocket with the stars and stripes painted on the side. Workers dash by with boxes of fireworks. LILA looks round, awed.

LILA: They look good...

CHULAK looks into LILA's cart.

CHULAK: Ours is good too. The displays so far haven't been anything special.

LILA: No, but Dr Puffenflasch and Sam Sparkington are next. They're the best.

CHULAK: You're doing something new.

LILA: (*Cheered.*) Yes. You're right. It will be different. Look at that prawn. Why's he got a prawn?

CHULAK: Don't you know? The King loves prawns.

LILA: Does he?

CHULAK: Prawn cocktail's his favourite. He loves it.

LILA: I've never heard that.

CHULAK: Mind you. It is nice.

The HUNGRY PIRATE's passing, carrying a box of Roman Candles.

HUNGRY PIRATE: I'll say. What I wouldn't do for a prawn cocktail. Or indeed any of the classic starters.

CHULAK: (*To HUNGRY PIRATE.*) What are you doing here?

CHANG struggles by with a Catherine Wheel.

CHANG: We're all here.

RAMBASHI appears with a rocket.

RAMBASHI: Chulak, my boy!

CHULAK: I thought you were singers.

RAMBASHI: Entertainers! It's all part of my plan.

HUNGRY PIRATE: Does the plan include food?

RAMBASHI: In time, in time.

CHULAK: This plan? Did it come to you in a flash?

RAMBASHI: (*Reeling with astonishment.*) How did you know that? It's a million rupee idea.

> (*Confidential.*)

> We're pretending to be temporary peripatetic workers but when everyone least expects it, we're going to burst into song. The King will be so impressed he'll almost certainly make us the Special and Particular Royal Entertainers. Especially when he hears our new song. It's about a special country far across the sea where Kings don't have to work so hard. It's a beautiful and mythical land, called a Republic.

CHULAK: I don't think you should sing that one, Uncle. The King's a bit unpredictable. He might put you in prison.

RAMBASHI: Don't worry my boy. I know what I'm doing.

HUNGRY PIRATE: Do you get fed in prison?

> *RAMBASHI hurries away.*

CHULAK: They'll get in trouble if they do that.

LILA: We're all in trouble. Look at these displays.

> *A trumpet announces the KING's arrival.*

CHULAK: The King!

> *The KING arrives with his SPECIAL AND PARTICULAR BODYGUARD dragging LALCHAND in chains. LILA wants to go to LALCHAND. CHULAK grabs her.*

CHULAK: No, Lila.

LILA: What have they done to him?

LALCHAND is thrown to the floor behind the KING. LILA gasps.

KING: We are ready for the final three displays. There is a prize of a gold cup and a thousand gold coins! The audience's applause will decide the winner.

The SPECIAL AND PARTICULAR BODYGUARD unveils a huge clapometer.

KING: Doctor Puffenflasch of Germany? Your display please?

DR. PUFFENFLASCH: Your excellency. It is my great pleasure to introduce my display entitled Bombardenorgelmitsparkenpumpe!

Dr. Puffenflasch pulls out a lighter that looks like a gun and starts his display. The finale involves the giant prawn blowing in two to reveal a prawn cocktail in a glass. This fizzes brilliantly. The King is clearly very impressed.

Dr. Puffenflasch takes his bow. The audience claps up to 9.0 on the clapometer.

LILA: That's a very high score.

CHULAK: I didn't think they'd like it that much.

KING: Colonel Sam Sparkington out of Alabama!

COLONEL SPARKINGTON: Your excellency. Prepare to be amazed, by the Southern Lights display!

COLONEL SAM SPARKINGTON strolls over to his rocket. He takes a match from his mouth, strikes it on his heel and tosses it at the fuse to the rocket. He then strolls off stage. The fuse for the rocket starts to splutter. Just before it's about to take off, COLONEL SAM runs onstage and leaps onto the back of the rocket. The rocket bucks and charges around the stage like a steer, but SAM holds onto a rein and refuses to be dislodged. Eventually, the rocket reaches the back of the stage where it whooshes off into space. COLONEL SAM is seen flying across the face of the moon. The crowd is awed for a moment then erupts into the most enormous applause. COLONEL SAM arrives for his bow, smouldering and dragging a charred parachute. The clapometer goes to 9.9.

CHULAK: (*Gulping.*) He can still be beaten. That wasn't even a proper display. It was just a big rocket. You've got big rockets too.

LILA: Not that big.

KING: Daughter of Lalchand the Firework-Maker!

CHULAK: Good luck, Lila.

LILA takes her bow.

LILA: Your excellency. I dedicate this display to my father, Lalchand, who's taught me everything.

LILA lights a long fuse leading to her display. The audience hushes. The fuse burns quickly to start the first firework. Just before it reaches the firework, it snuffs and dies.

CHULAK: Relight it. Quick.

LILA: I can't.

CHULAK: Why not?

LILA: It's too close to the firework. It'll blow me to pieces. I have to fit a new fuse.

The KING stands up.

KING: Kill him!

The crowd gasps. LALCHAND is dragged by the SPECIAL AND PARTICULAR BODYGUARD to an execution block with a sword at his throat.

LILA: No!

CHULAK grabs LILA and shakes her.

CHULAK: Fit a new fuse. Quickly! I'll hold him up!

CHULAK jumps out in front of the KING.

CHULAK: Your excellent and kind Majesty. Before you execute the traitor...

The KING glares at CHULAK. The SPECIAL AND PARTICULAR BODYGUARD bends LALCHAND over the block and prepares to behead him. The KING holds up a hand to stop the execution.

CHULAK: In honour of your great wisdom and generosity, and in celebration of your many glorious years, I would like to show you some wondrous... Juggling!

CHULAK starts juggling and clowning.

KING: Enough! I said kill him!

The KING turns to the SPECIAL AND PARTICULAR BODYGUARD. LILA throws herself on the floor with a lighter.

LILA: (*Diving for cover.*) Your Majesty! My display!

LILA takes control of the display, pointing to the fireworks as they explode. She's in her element, a natural, a master. When it's finished there's a long and deadly silence.

COLONEL SAM stands.

COLONEL SPARKINGTON: (*Throwing hat in air.*) Yeeee-har!

DR. PUFFENFLASCH: Hoch, hoch, hoch!

There's deafening applause. The clapometer goes round to 10 and then continues, spinning out of control until it explodes and shoots smoke out of the top. There are cheers and LILA is picked up and carried round on the shoulders of the crowd. LILA is swamped by the other Firework-Makers.

DR. PUFFENFLASCH: Your display was magnificent.

COLONEL SPARKINGTON: What're you putting in them there rockets. I ain't never seen nothing like it. We've got to talk, lady.

DR. PUFFENFLASCH: Jah! I would be honoured if you would both join me for a sausage dinner.

LILA: Thank you. I too would be honoured.

KING: Silence!

The celebrations cease.

KING: The girl lit a firework that went out. By the rules of the competition she is disqualified.

The crowd hiss. There's a few boos.

DR. PUFFENFLASCH: Please your majesty. The girl is the winner...

COLONEL SPARKINGTON: Darn right she is. That was some display.

The KING stares until the crowd is cowed into silence. There'll be no revolt against this KING.

KING: I say when the competition is over. I decide the winner.

Silence.

KING: I'm glad that's understood.

The SPECIAL AND PARTICULAR BODYGUARD holds LALCHAND by the hair as he awaits the KING's order. The KING looks over. LALCHAND is about to die.

KING: I have decided to overlook this technicality. The girl has won! Free the Firework-Maker!

The SPECIAL AND PARTICULAR BODYGUARD kicks LALCHAND away from the execution block and he escorts the KING away. LILA picks up the golden cup and her thousand crowns. There's a huge cheer.

LILA breaks away to speak to CHULAK who's with RAMBASHI.

RAMBASHI: Chulak my boy! It's a million rupee idea. I'm the manager, you're the lead singer. My boys are the backing band. We'll call you Chulak and the Chickens.

CHULAK: I'd like that.

RAMBASHI off.

LILA: Is that a good idea?

CHULAK: I think so.

LILA: I mean the terrible name?

RAMBASHI: It's not terrible. What could be more noble than a hen?

CHULAK: You're the champion.

LILA: I couldn't have done it without you and Hamlet. Where is Hamlet?

CHULAK: He's with Frangipani. She liked him all along - she was just shy.

HAMLET and FRANGIPANI appear.

HAMLET: Well done Lila. I knew you'd win.

LILA: Thanks Hamlet. Nice to meet you Frangipani.

HAMLET: She can play the saxophone. She can't speak. What do you want from us? We're elephants!

RAMBASHI: Chulak!

LILA: I need to speak to my father.

CHULAK goes. LILA sees LALCHAND. They move to the front of the stage as everyone else leaves in the background.

LALCHAND: Lila, my dear, will you accept my apology?

LILA: Do I need to?

LALCHAND: I didn't trust you. I should have. You have the Three Gifts.

LILA: I don't even know what they are.

LALCHAND: They're what all Firework-Makers must have. They are equally important, and two of them are no good without the third. The first one is talent, and you have that, my dear.

LILA: Thank you.

LALCHAND: The second has many names: courage, determination, will-power... It's what made you carry on climbing the mountain when everything seemed hopeless.

LILA: And the third?

LALCHAND: Luck. It gave you good friends like Chulak and Hamlet, and brought them to you in time. Those are the Three Gifts, and you took them and offered them to Razvani as a Firework-Maker should. And he gave you the Royal Sulphur in exchange.

LILA: No, he didn't.

LALCHAND: It's not a substance. I tricked you on that. The golden pot with the green lid-

LILA: Isn't Royal Sulphur.

LALCHAND: (*Disappointed.*) You knew?

LILA: Of course.

LALCHAND: I thought it might give you a little confidence...

LILA: You did it out of love. It gave me strength. What is Royal Sulphur?

LALCHAND: You've more Royal Sulphur than I'll ever have... It's wisdom. You gain it by suffering and risk - by taking the journey to Mount Merapi and walking into the flames. It's what the journey is for. Each of our friends the other Firework-Makers has made his own journey in a similar way, and so have Rambashi and Chulak. You didn't come home empty-handed, Lila. You brought back the Royal Sulphur.

LILA: I see...

LALCHAND: You know what this means?

LILA: What does it mean?

LALCHAND: It means you're a Firework-Maker.

LILA: *Now*, I see.

> *LILA throws up her hand and a huge spray of silver covers the two of them. There's a small explosion. They've disappeared.*
>
> *The End.*